About the Author

In this book, the Congolese artist Faida Tshimwanga (Jovanie) publishes her vision of restoring world peace through a respectful approach to human rights and democracy. Jovanie underwent an epiphany while reading one of the greatest novels of the 19 century: *Les Misérables* by Victor Hugo. After finishing the novel, she found herself overcome with emotion because saying goodbye to Cosette was like saying farewell to a mirror filled with the same stories of poverty and misery that she was all too familiar with. The novel inspired her to pursue and develop her own creative talents. Through those talents, she would then share her story with the world.

A New Era with Cosette

Faida Tshimwanga

A New Era with Cosette

Olympia Publishers
London

www.olympiapublishers.com
OLYMPIA PAPERBACK EDITION

Copyright © Faida Tshimwanga 2024

The right of Faida Tshimwanga to be identified as author of
this work has been asserted in accordance with sections 77 and 78 of
the Copyright, Designs and Patents Act 1988.

All Rights Reserved

No reproduction, copy or transmission of this publication
may be made without written permission.
No paragraph of this publication may be reproduced,
copied or transmitted save with the written permission of the publisher,
or in accordance with the provisions
of the Copyright Act 1956 (as amended).

Any person who commits any unauthorised act in relation to
this publication may be liable to criminal
prosecution and civil claims for damage.

A CIP catalogue record for this title is
available from the British Library.

ISBN: 978-1-80439-047-4

This is a work of fiction.
Names, characters, places and incidents originate from the writer's
imagination. Any resemblance to actual persons, living or dead, is
purely coincidental.

First Published in 2024

Olympia Publishers
Tallis House
2 Tallis Street
London
EC4Y 0AB

Printed in Great Britain

Dedication

I dedicate this book to Victor Hugo.

Acknowledgements

Thank you, Cosette, for the book *Les Misérables* by Victor Hugo gave me the inspiration to write this book.

Chap 1

*The Devil
with
Adam and Eve*

1. Universe

The beginning of God,
the devil, the people.
Flowers, animals,
the sun, the moon,
the storm, the rain,
the sky, the earth
and the music.

2. Universe

The angels, the smile, the light, the shadow,
the tears, the joy, the melancholy, the breathing,
the wind, the feelings
and
the emotions.
This includes everything that can be found
or
felt in our world,
such as
people themselves,
life, love, the good, the bad, the geometric shapes
and
the numbers.

3. Universe

These include the beginning of creation;
the seas, the lakes, the forests,
the emptiness, the colours, the death,
the dreams, the thoughts,
the climate and the infinity…

4. Adam and Eve

Ancestors were driven out of the garden of Eden
by
God because of the devil.
The devil deceived them,
so
they ate the fruit forbidden by God.
They ate this fruit
and
found themselves lost
and
all alone outside of paradise.

Chap 2

Cosette
with
Elima 1 et Elima 2

5. Cosette

A woman as a symbol of all women of the World.
She wondered how she could bring peace.
She wants to create a world where
The people are available to find solutions
to all their problems
so that
people would live in the world without the devil.
Cosette had always wanted love and
peace between the people.
The woman named Cosette represents all women of our world.
regardless of their skin color.
She was the union of all women in the world.

6. The Reactions

1. Face has the mouth wide open.
This colour is heavenly
and
says that his knowledge of God comes from Heaven.
2. There is another face with black paint
which
covers one eye,
and
symbolises ignorance.
3. Red face is located between the first
and the
second because it's incapable
of
a decision; it always follows the instructions of others.

7. Elima 1

Elima is an evil spirit sent by the devil,
so
she brings fear among the people.
This spirit lives in the water.

8. Elima 2

Elima 2 against its will is also in the service
of
the devil and lives in the water.
The devil sent her to visit a woman called Cosette.

9. Horror

That is Cosette;
when she saw with her own eyes
the evil spirits Elima 1 *et* Elima 2,
she screamed in terror.

10. Cosette in Trance

It's in a hypnotic state;
she swayed between the two worlds.
She had once in life encouraged the spirits Elima 1 and
Elima 2,
these spirits who live in water were sent by the devil to scare
Cosette.
When Cosette saw the two spirits,
she screamed horror
and
fell into a trance.

Chap 3

*Cosette
and
the Souls of Hell*

11. These Souls Are the Souls

These souls are the souls who live in Hell,
but at
the moment, they were trying to walk
for only a few minutes outside
of
Hell
and
yet return to where they came from.
Cosette met these souls on her way,
and
they accompanied her to Hell.

12. Hell

This is Hell where poor souls suffer;
the unhappy souls are being owned by fire day by day.
This is very sad and pathetic.
Hell is the kingdom of the devil
and
his demons.

the souls suffer to pursue the path of evil.

At this moment,
Cosette entered Hell and saw with her own eyes
the atrocious suffering of souls in Hell?
Cosette decided to help these poor souls.

13. A Cry of a Soul

A cry of suffering emitted from a soul,
so that someone could come to its aid.
This was a soul of Hell.
She needed help because
she could no longer endure the suffering
of
Hell, which was caused
by
the devil and his demons.

14. The Cries of Souls

These souls were crying
because
they needed liberation.
Those souls in Hell felt the presence
of
a human being
and
this person was indeed Cosette.
The souls were convinced
that
this woman Cosette could save them despite
suffering caused by the devil and his demons.

Chap 4

The Cosette Mask

15. The Cosette Mask

That is the transformation
of
Cosette as a mask.
The devil had seen that Cosette would save the souls of Hell
and so
he transformed Cosette into a mask so that
she could not save anyone.
The devil secretly contaminated the Cosette Mask
with
a disease called Zebola.

16. The Gate of a Soul

It is the eye that allows us to read
the thoughts of other people.
The eye is also the gateway of a soul.
The soul of Cosette lived
in
Hell,
with
the view of eyes
and
she returned to the Earth.

17. The Masked Cosette's Zebola

The poor Cosette returned
to
the world of human beings
but
became a mask;
she was also suffering from a disease called Zebola.
Cosette sought the cure…

Chap 5

Zebola Disease

18. Cosette with the Zebola

Cosette was returned to her body
but
she was still suffering from the disease, Zebola.
Zebola is a mysterious disease
in
the Democratic Republic of Congo.
This sickness is traditionally treated
as
she descended from devils, demons or sorcery.
When a person suffers from this sickness,
she or he becomes like a mad man.
It's said a person who suffers from Zebola will lose
consciousness
and
their memories.
This allows evil spirits to communicate through the person's
body.

In the case of Cosette,
she didn't know
where
she was,
and
where
she came from,

because
she had lost consciousness
and
the devil made Cosette to be like a madwoman.

Chap 6

Cosette and the Fetishist

19. Cosette and the Shaman

Cosette began living with the shaman
so
he could treat her
and
free her from this evil disease Zebola, which can only be
treated by a traditional doctor.
The witch doctors communicate
with spirits.
The spirits then guide the witch doctors
to cure patients.
These doctors are called "Nganga nkisi" in Lingala language.
As
Cosette suffered the devil,
the demons enjoyed her suffering.
The devil is pure evil,
he doesn't have any right to be in our world.
Therefore, we will haunt him forever.

20. The "Zebola" Dance by Cosette

The Satanic spirits tormented Cosette further.
She started spirit dancing. Cosette hoped that by dancing the evil spirit could free themselves.
Over four months,
she got treatments for the cure but the poor Cosette could not recover.
The devil denied her the ability
to regain health, even with the effort provided by the witch doctors.
With
the spiritual dance, Cosette confronted the spirits.
The spirits communicate the messages and transfer these messages to the people;
with
Zebola, Cosette became a messenger of the devil's thoughts to the living.

Chap 7

Cosette and the Shaman

21. The Death of Cosette

Finally, due to the illness, Zebola, and despite efforts on the
part of the witch doctor,
Cosette could not resist the demons that disturbed her day
and night
and
she found death.
The devil, demons as well as his whole kingdom killed
Cosette in a mysterious way.
Cosette loved all people without any discrimination;
any nationality, skin colour, gender, class, language, religion
or
political opinion.
She did not want to see people suffering.
Her most sincere wish was that all people could live in
harmony with each other.
Cosette had noted that all people have a common point that
unites us;
the blood that flows in our veins.
Cosette always wanted the five continents united,
and
the five continents would speak only the love language.
Cosette died to liberate humanity from the clutches
of
the devil and evil.
The devil himself killed Cosette in mysterious ways
so that
he could have a hold on people.

Chap 8

The Closure of Hell

22. The Negotiation between Cosette and the Devil

After her death, Cosette met God,
and
she asked God to forgive the devil.
His demons
and
sorcerers in the sky could be reinstated
and
leave the humanity on Earth in peace.
God accepted the proposal by Cosette
so that the devil could return to the sky.
Cosette then met the devil
and
proposed to him to leave Hell forever and that he must
return with all demons and sorcerers to the sky.
The devil long thought about the proposal of Cosette and he
accepted finally to return to Heaven, because
God had forgiven him.
The devil accepted again
to become an angel.

23. The Closure of Hell

The devil organised the closing of the Hell
and
Cosette monitored the collection of all evil spirits,
which were on the Earth; in water,
in
the forests, so that she could be sure
that no devil still lived on the Earth.
Cosette also worked after her death.
The day had come when the devil would drive his entire
Satanic kingdom in the sky.
Cosette closed the Hell forever.
The devil, the demons and
sorcerers ascended into Heaven
and
they became angels once more.
Now, the global rebirth began.
This global rebirth began on 9 August 2013 in Togo Lomé.

Chap 9

A New Era
A World Without the Devil,
Heaven on Earth

24. A New Epoque

A world without the devil, Heaven on Earth.
On 9 August 2013, in Togo Lomé,
the world started to live in non-existence
of
the devil. Our children will know nothing more
of
the devil because the issues
of
the devil have ended.
Now we will tell our children only about the existence
of
angels, joy,
love and peace.

Chap 10

The Souls of Paradise

25, 26, 27. The Souls of Paradise

The souls of paradise are the souls
of
the whole world which are all united on the earthly paradise;
that means, you, me, we, all of us are the souls of paradise.

Chap 11

The Red People

28. The Red People

The Red People are the inhabitants
of
earthly paradise because
our common point is the blood that circulates in our bodies.
We share the love between us in which we exhale.
If
I take a breath,
I take in the love from people all over the world;
when I breathe out,
I give my love to all the people in the world.
Through inhale and exhale, we share our love with each
other
so that
our paradise on Earth can become a reality.

29. Fusion

All human beings are naturally united by the circulation of their blood.

30. The World of Peace

Finally, the smile of the new era is here. I am extremely happy to live in a paradise on Earth. All the people in the world, let us celebrate happily our paradise on Earth.

I beg you to promote joy, love and peace.

Painting Exhibition
"A New Era with Cosette" in Togo Lomé, 9 August 2013,
by Artist Jovanie

I was inspired by the character Cosette from the book *Les Misérables* by Victor Hugo.